Thurrock

in old picture postcards

Thurrock
in old picture postcards

Published with the co-operation of Thurrock Borough Council,
Leisure Services Division, Essex, England
K.E. Fryer, Leisure Services Manager

European Library   ZALTBOMMEL / THE NETHERLANDS

This publication includes: Aveley, Bulphan, Chadwell, Corringham, Fobbing, Grays, Horndon, Langdon Hills, Mucking, Orsett, Ockendon, Stanford, Stifford, the Tilburys, West Thurrock and Purfleet.

GB ISBN 90 288 3071 5

© 1984 European Library – Zaltbommel/The Netherlands

Ninth edition, 1998: reprint of the original edition of 1984.

INTRODUCTION

Just over a hundred years ago, in 1882, the local trade directories listed for the first time a photographer's studio in Grays — Turner Jessop's in New Road. Soon afterwards Jessop was advertising 'Architectural and Out-Door Photographs in all Sizes', which, together with numerous portrait pictures, he continued to produce until his death in 1920. Through Jessop's period, other notable local photographers had emerged to make their mark also. Around 1900, C.M. Ansell of South Ockendon, produced a souvenir booklet of village views around his home, while town photographers, such as Alfred Russell of Orsett Road, S. Edwin of Clarence Road, and William Menlove of Whitehall Lane, all developed images which survive to recreate the look of our district in the early-twentieth century.

In 1916 'The Camera as Historian' had been published, a popular book which soon created a wider awareness of film as means of preserving some record of our cultural heritage, landscape, costume and architecture. Christopher Shiner, a notable architect of the growing town at this period, was to take up this theme with the Grays and District Photographic Society. In the autumn of 1922, he addressed the Society — then in its second season of activity — with a reminder of the value of photographs 'in keeping records of towns like Grays, which were constantly changing'.

To many readers, this book will have a primary appeal for its nostalgic quality, and certainly — looking through its scenes — it is easy to imagine a cosier, less complicated, more idyllic past which once supposedly happened. But it also has great value for the objective historian as an accurate record of workaday conditions and environment. Pictures like these can give the only evidence we have of important mediaeval buildings that are now lost, of local methods of agricultural work, or of the style of costume worn by a Tilbury Hotel chambermaid in the Edwardian era.

The district which this book examines is today called Thurrock, a name already known at the close of the Saxon period. *Turroc* was a topographically descriptive name, — likening the meandering of the Thames to the bottom curve of a boat's framework. Three parishes, through post-conquest years, were carved out from the great Saxon estate of Turroc. These became in time called Grays Thurrock, West Thurrock and Little Thurrock. But not until 1936 was a wider area to assume the overall identity of the old Saxon placename — as the Thurrock Urban District. Its design was a natural one, embracing about 65 square miles of river clays, light uplands and fen pasture, and nearly twenty villages that hinged to the old market towns of Orsett, Grays and Horndon. Under the Poor Law Amendment Act of 1834, Orsett — the most central — had been seen as the logical hub to this circle of communities and subsequently the whole of what is now called *Thurrock* had been administered — so far as welfare services were concerned — by the Guardians of the Poor for the Orsett Union. Thurrock's identity as a Local Government area had therefore existed in embryo for over a century by the time of reorganisation in 1936.

It is from the second half of that century that these photographs largely come, a period of significant change in which the impact of mechanised industry struck — and quickly overtook — a rural society. And some of the photographic images which follow illustrate this change very forcibly.

The reasons behind Thurrock's metamorphosis were many. Local geology and technological advance are perhaps its essential keys. For upwards of 10,000 years basic mineral resources had been locally exploited; flint, salt, chalk and clays were all processed in the district for moderate human needs between prehistoric and mediaeval times. Before 1600 opencast limestone mining had cut away the Purfleet hillslopes. By 1760 a bold scheme of land reclamation was even underway on the same site, to level and re-fill disused quarry workings with gunpowder storage sheds.

Through this same Purfleet chalk-bluff the London, Tilbury and Southend Railway advanced in 1854, consuming not only huge local gravel resources in its progress, but exploiting geology more simply — through track-laying across the level miles of Thames flood-plain. By 1856 all of the district had become a viable scenario for industrial penetration, offering abundant minerals, tidal waters and now an iron track.

Though the railway had been conceived largely as a holiday line for the expanding pleasure-ground of Southend, local enterprise would be quick to exploit its benefits. Purfleet's waterfront even developed something of a 'seaside' atmosphere and shaped itself as an East-Londoner's resort, its only hotel, 'Wingroves', gaining a certain notoriety in Victorian divorce dramas. A later offshoot of the railway's effect on Purfleet was the use of discarded chalk-workings for the filming of cinema movies — especially British 'westerns'. Closeness to the metropolitan studios, a choice of romantic locations and minimum rainfall — less than twenty inches annually — doubtless contributed to the popularity of the district for these shoe-string productions.

But three *major* industries were to be the forces that changed an agricultural face; cement and concrete production in Thurrock's western quarter, docks in the central zone and oil storage depots upon its eastern marshes around the creeks of Shellhaven. Beginning in the 1870's with the expansion of Grays town as centre of cement production, new housing developments over the next century would extend across many square miles, linking into one urban strand the riverine fringes of West Thurrock, Grays, Little Thurrock and Chadwell and later uniting Stanford-le-Hope and Corringham into upland estate-towns. Post-war re-settlement of London's population likewise absorbed much of the high farmland of South Ockendon and Aveley. Today no Thurrock villages survive solely as agricultural communities, though West Tilbury — despite spectacular electricity power stations on its marshland — is essentially rural in mood and activity.

The shift from agricultural employment to factory and dock labour which rocketed locally from the 1880's, was largely enforced by a phase of economic decline. South Essex had long been a corn-producing country. Its tenant farmers, confident in a continuation of profit in cereals, awoke too late to the realisation that steam technology had caught up on them. Ships could now deliver prairie wheat more cheaply from Canada or America than it could be grown at home. The story of the collapse is well documented, as is its sequel of Scottish and West Country dairy-men migrating to revitalize the neglected and weed-infested acres of the Orsett Union. The pastoral immigrants required little labour other than that provided by their own families. Large workforces of men, women and children, so necessary to arable farming systems, were, for Essex, a feature of the past.

The devaluation of local farmland in the depression years tempted landlords to selling outright, or at least severely rationalising their estates. One of the largest landed proprietors, for example, relinquished valuable chalk-lands at South Stifford to the growing cement industry. At Chadwell, a smaller proprietor, Daniel Jackson, grasped the opportunity of the moment to sign over marshland to the East and West India Dock Company. The year was 1882. Within a decade these Chadwell clays would be transformed under tidal docks and a new town — called 'Tilbury' because the development lay closer to Tilbury Fort than any other significant landmark. The jobless rural worker hurried to the machine and the tenement block.

Against this background, population leapt as immigrants were either individually attracted or — as in the Boer War munitions drive — posted in from other distant factories. The engineering of docks at Tilbury effected a rise of population in Chadwell, within one decade, from 587 rural inhabitants to well over 3,000 riverside workers. Another 2,000 had arrived there by 1901. Corringham trebled its small population between 1890 and 1910. Largely due to cement and stock brick production, Grays increased from around 2,000 people in 1861 to over 13,000 by the century's turn. A framework was set for this to become the main town of the district. The stability of numbers in agricultural villages off the industrialist's map provides a marked contrast at the very same time; Horndon-on-the-Hill harboured a steady 500 or 600 people through the Victorian age and Mucking remained equally stable at around 250. Orsett — especially amid the depression years — even declined slightly in population.

Despite a return to agricultural stability the crippling of the landed families who had owned so much of Thurrock was virtually complete by 1930. Through this time, increasing demands for chalk, gravel and clays encouraged further releases to industry for exploitation of the landscape. At Stanford-le-Hope and Mucking, hundreds of agricultural acres — including ancient farmhouses and unrecorded archaeological settlements — would be destroyed following planning consents made in the early-1930's. At a similar period, marshland dumping of domestic refuse began on a major scale eastward of Tilbury Fort, while concurrently the Bata Shoe enterprise moved onto newly purchased territory inland. By 1938, this firm had created a model factory-town complete with home-farm, orchards, cinema and impressive hotel across the fields of the mediaeval St. Clere's Hall.

In this book, the fundamental note is therefore one of contrast. We are looking sometimes at country people who lived at the perimeter of industrial complexity — and possibly even engaged in factory employment. Conversely, in the urban pictures — with their bandstands, gasometers and heavy plant — the countryside and its old-fashioned requirements may only be a few hundred yards away. For centuries, our district had been injected with Kentish and East Anglian migrant families. Its girls, since at least the Stuart age, had borne off-spring by garrison soldiers from many other regions. They intermarried with Dutch engineers and labourers. By 1890 Irish accents were probably more frequently heard south of Orsett than any Essex pronunciation. Russians were present in Corringham during the period of the Kynoch explosive factory operation, while in East Tilbury — even today — Czechoslovakian traits among the villagers will be easily observed. Truly this Thameside region has, for a diverse array of working people over many years, been 'a land of beginning again'.

Since the inception of its photo-archive in 1975, the Thurrock Museums Service has added to its collections at a steady rate of over a thousand photographs per year. Many pictures — especially Edwardian commercial postcards — have kindly been loaned by local people during this programme for copying onto negative film, and to all those who have assisted, the Museum is greatly indebted. Especially helpful to the creation of this book have been Mrs. V. Ashdown of Chadwell St. Mary, the S. and B. Picture Library of Grays Thurrock, and Gordon Hales Esq. of Tilbury, all of whom also gave information useful to the text. Production of the finished prints and captions was by Terry Carney, Assistant Curator.

Randal Bingley

1. CORRINGHAM. But for the dress of the two children, which places this picture about 1910, we could be looking at a view from the earliest years of photography. The motor-car and modern road surfaces have greatly changed villages like Corringham, although this scene is still recognisable. At the end of the row is 'The Bull Inn', and to the right of it stands a pair of sixteenth century cottages near the entrance to Hall Farm. The buildings next to 'The Bull' have been demolished to make a car-park, but the rest of the group has survived without any major alterations.

2. THE 'ROYAL HOTEL', PURFLEET. This carefully composed picture is a perfect evocation of Edwardian Purfleet as experienced by its many visitors. The 'Royal Hotel' had been built early in the nineteenth century on the site of an older inn called 'The Ship'. It had itself been known as 'The Bricklayers Arms', 'The Purfleet Hotel', and 'Wingrove's Hotel', before the management decided to call it 'Royal' on the strength of visits by Edward VII when Prince of Wales. On the right of this photograph is one of several tea-rooms which provided refreshment for the less prosperous visitors who came on special excursion trains from East London.

3. ORSETT LAUNDRY. This photograph, which is not a commercial postcard, appears to show the entire staff of this local laundry business about 1900. Before the domestic washing machine came into general use it was not unusual for even relatively poor families to send their washing to one of the many small laundries of this type which generally made very modest charges. This particular business at Orsett, quite a small village, probably obtained much of its work from the Orsett Union Workhouse which stood on the site now occupied by the Orsett Hospital.

The Wharf
Stanford le Hope

4. THE WHARF, STANFORD-LE-HOPE. An attractive picture in its own right, this is also a valuable record of the long abandoned Stanford Wharf, now barely recognisable on the ground though commemorated in 'Wharf Road' which once connected it to the centre of the village. Beyond the graceful lines of a Thames sailing barge, the cluster of wharfside buildings includes a large barn almost filled with hay, a product which along with grain was often transported by barge. In 1930 the Stanford fire brigade were called to a fire in a granary at the wharf, but it had apparently been empty for some time.

5. TILBURY DOCK FOUNDATION STONE CEREMONY. A historically important photograph dating from the earliest years of the Tilbury Docks which opened in 1886. It was taken by R. Hider of Gravesend for the engineers involved in the operation, Messrs. Whitaker Bros. of Horsforth, Leeds, and is captioned 'Laying the Heel Post Stone at Tilbury Docks'. The large block of stone can be seen in the background suspended on chains, ready to be lowered into the hole prepared for it. An interesting social range appears in this picture which includes senior officials of the East and West India Docks Company, the labourers who actually did the work, and a policeman.

The Rectory West Tilbury.

6. THE RECTORY, WEST TILBURY. The Reverend Reuben Fellows stands among the trees and shrubs of his garden on the north side of the parsonage at West Tilbury. The building had once been an inn called 'The New King's Head', which was refashioned as a rectory at the end of the eighteenth century. It was considerably extended in the Victorian period to create the large residence shown here about 1930. Mr. Fellows had formerly been rector of East Tilbury, but in 1918 obtained in addition the living at West Tilbury and used regularly to cycle between his two churches. The rectory was demolished in 1965.

7. HARVESTERS AT HORNDON-ON-THE-HILL. The precise location of this attractive picture has not been established, but there is good evidence that it was taken in Horndon-on-the-Hill around 1910. The photographer, perhaps partly to keep the men still, has posed four of them leaning on their scythes, apparently in the act of sharpening the blades, although one of them has still managed to move his head. A fifth man is holding an earthenware beer flagon and a horn cup to demonstrate the form of refreshment that was traditional on these occasions. He is probably the 'stooker' who would bind the corn cut by the others.

Stanford le Hope

8. STANFORD-LE-HOPE. Instantly recognisable to those who know Stanford, this view from the Hassenbrook bridge shows on the left the buildings of Boorman's corn mill, which were demolished in 1964. A horse-drawn cart can be seen at its entrance. Further along the road is the Railway Tavern with a sign advertising Ind Coope's Romford Ales. Originally a seventeenth century building, it was well known at this period (around 1910) for its auction room where sales were conducted by Messrs. Offin and Rumsey. The Railway Tavern has survived, but unfortunately the trees, which contribute so much to this pleasant scene, have not.

9. LARKIN'S CORNER, ORSETT. This crossroads in Orsett village is still known as Larkin's Corner after the weatherboarded house called Larkin's in the centre of this early-morning photograph. The house, which is itself named after a former owner or tenant, is of the hall and crosswing type, and is probably of late-mediaeval origin. It was, however, greatly altered during the 1960's and no longer gives such an impression of antiquity. The road continues between the trees towards Bulphan, while the turning on the right leads to Orsett Hall. The bicycles of the photographer and his assistant can be seen by the signpost.

10. W.P. WALKER, IRONMONGERS OF GRAYS. Shop-fronts were popular subjects for Edwardian postcards, but this one has been selected for its particularly fine display of goods, both in the windows and on the pavement. The building, now demolished, occupied a prominent corner site at the junction of Maidstone Road and the High Street. In the windows are bird cages, metal trays and containers, brushes and knives, while outside there are rolls of wire netting, scythe handles, and garden furniture. The painted sign by the door advertises various electrical fittings, electricity not being in sufficiently wide use at this time to justify specialist shops.

11. SOUTH OCKENDON FOOTBALL CLUB, 1919-1920. Photographs of sports teams do not usually make much impact, but this one gains from the inclusion of South Ockendon's most distinctive landmark, the parish church with its thirteenth century round tower, a feature not uncommon elsewhere in East Anglia, particularly Norfolk, but rare in Essex. The picture also records the site of the local football pitch, immediately to the south of the church. Places like South Ockendon had more distinct identities at this time with consequently stronger support for the local team in matches with neighbouring villages than we might find today.

12. THE SEA WALL AT PURFLEET. This photograph was taken in the 1890's, to record the effects of exceptionally high tides. The three gentlemen appear to be examining a break in the sea wall and the flooding that this has caused. Moored in the river is the training ship 'Cornwall' which was at Purfleet from 1868 until 1928. Like other training ships in the area, 'Cornwall' was established for the education of boys with a view to their joining the Navy, but differed from them in being a reformatory ship. Its band was a familiar sight at parades and special events in the district. On the right hand side of the picture in the far distance, the shape of the 'Royal Hotel' can just be distinguished.

The Rookery, Stanford-le-Hope.

13. THE ROOKERY, STANFORD-LE-HOPE. This early Georgian red brick house still stands on the main London to Southend Road just outside the built-up part of modern Stanford, although it is no longer covered in ivy. It was built in 1735 by James Adams who named it 'New Jenkins'. Some time after his death in 1765, it was re-named 'Adamsley', and appears under this name on the 1777 map of Essex by Chapman and André. We see from this photograph that in the early part of the present century it was 'The Rookery', and in recent years it has been 'St. Clere's Hall', a name transferred from another house at East Tilbury, now demolished. Whatever we call it, it is a fine building.

The Harrow, Bulphan

128319

14. THE HARROW, BULPHAN. Surrounded by fields and a considerable distance from the village, this is a strangely remote site for a public house. It must have relied first on the bicycle and then on the motor-car to bring its customers out here for a drink in the country. Bulphan's low-lying fenland had long been a prime cattle-grazing area, but by the 1930's, poultry farmers and nurserymen had also become established in the district. This picture of about 1930 shows an attractive sign in the form of a miniature harrow. The licensee at this time was Mrs. Ellen Thomas.

43435. TILBURY DRY DOCK.

15. TILBURY DRY DOCK. A picture which recalls Tilbury's long association with the Orient Line Shipping Company. The liner 'Ophir', built in 1891, was an Orient Line ship of 6,814 tons, which in 1901 had the distinction of being chartered by the Admiralty for use as a royal yacht on a world tour by the Duke and Duchess of York (later to become King George V and Queen Mary). This photograph was probably taken after the royal tour, but before the 'Ophir' was requisitioned for use as an armed cruiser in 1914. It later became a hospital ship and was finally broken up in 1922.

16. STIFFORD. A view of one of the district's more picturesque villages, taken during the 1930's. Even today Stifford preserves some of this rural charm, many of its cottages having kept their thatch and old world character. The cottage in the hollow on the right is a seventeenth century building with later additions, while the taller building on the left, also built in the seventeenth century, was original-ly an inn called 'The Oaks'. Long before this photograph was taken it was divided into three cottages.

17. TILBURY POST OFFICE. The Post and Telegraph Office at No. 1 Dock Road must have been one of the first substantial buildings constructed to meet the needs of the new town of Tilbury in the 1880's. With its classical touches around the door and windows it was clearly designed to impress. Henry Alfred Suggett, baker and confectioner, took over the building as postmaster in 1889 and appears in this picture of about 1905, surrounded by his shop and postal staff. About this time there were three deliveries and four collections daily, with the post office open from 7 a.m. to 9 p.m.

18. WINDMILL AT SOUTH OCKENDON. This smock mill was, until 1977, a prominent feature of the landscape, having stood on this open and slightly elevated site at South Ockendon since the beginning of the nineteenth century, although there is good evidence that a mill was operating here as early as the thirteenth century. The photograph was taken around 1900 when the mill was still in use, and the photographer was almost certainly C.M. Ansell, whose book of views of North and South Ockendon was published about this time. In the foreground is the water-filled moat of South Ockendon Hall, a mediaeval building long since demolished.

19. ORSETT ROAD, GRAYS. Orsett Road had not long been a shopping area when this picture was taken around 1910. Before 1900 the road was essentially residential, and the large Victorian houses to the right of the shops recall its former character. The picture is full of interesting details: the board announcing a newspaper report of the free meals debate, advertisements for cigarettes and chocolate, a poster for the Grand Theatre, and a small plough for sale on the pavement. Of the three shops, E.V. Saxton, G. Cockley, and G.E. Gilbert, only Saxtons are still trading on the same site, and they no longer offer 'Haircutting, Shaving and Shampooing'.

20. CORRINGHAM CHURCH. This corner of old Corringham has fortunately escaped serious altera-
tion, and a very similar picture could be taken today. The church, dedicated to St. Mary, is mainly of
the fourteenth century, but it has a late Saxon or early Norman tower, and is architecturally one of
the most interesting in the borough. The three men with their dog, gun, and cat, add interest to an
otherwise ordinary picture. Perhaps the photographer found them in 'The Bull Inn' opposite and
persuaded them to leave their lunchtime drinks for a few moments.

21. BELMONT CASTLE, GRAYS. This photograph, probably by the Grays photographer, Alfred Russell, was taken in the 1930's, sadly the last years of this elegant building. Belmont Castle was built about 1795 to a design by Thomas Jeffery for the local landowner Zachariah Button. It was in the fashionable gothic style of the day, and is one of the district's most serious losses, having been demolished in 1943 to make way for chalk extraction. Originally surrounded by well kept lawns, and with unobstructed views across the Thames, it must have seemed more and more incongruous as dull Edwardian terraces and modern industry advanced towards it.

22. ROSE COTTAGE. This local landmark is often recalled by West Thurrock residents although it was demolished many years ago. It stood at the junction of Mill Lane and London Road, and its rose-covered walls must have done much to raise the spirits of passers-by at a time when industrial developments were changing the area so dramatically. Although the brick exterior was of early-nineteenth century date, there was almost certainly an older building underneath. The picture was taken about 1910 when a wide range of modern industries, symbolised here by the distant chimneys, were well established in West Thurrock.

Oxford Street Langdon Hills

124930

23. OXFORD STREET, LANGDON HILLS. Only the clothing of the fashionably dressed lady and her children places this picture firmly in the 1920's. Langdon Hills with its elevated situation and wooded slopes must always have seemed different from the rest of Thurrock. It has changed little since this photograph was taken, and as much of the area consists of country parks administered by the County Council, its future is probably assured. The name 'Oxford Street' was once attached to the road now known as Lee Chapel Lane, and in view of the associations Oxford Street has for most people, it was probably a good idea to change it.

24. THE PRINCE ALBERT, AVELEY. A picture full of interest and activity, although the actual occasion is not known. A crowd has gathered outside 'The Prince Albert' in Aveley High Street, some of its members no doubt waiting for it to open on a Sunday lunchtime. There has clearly been some kind of parade, since best clothes, sashes, and musical instruments are much in evidence, together with a policeman to keep order. The Prince Albert, an old inn which in the previous century had changed its name to that of the Queen's consort, was part of the Seabrookes' empire, and the 'Thurrock' ales of the Grays brewery are boldly advertised on its walls.

MANOR FARM,
STANFORD le HOPE.

25. MANOR FARM, STANFORD-LE-HOPE. This moated farmhouse stood in the area known as 'The Warren' at Stanford-le-Hope, a short distance to the north of the footpath across the marshes. The farmhouse, formerly known as Cabborns, was essentially a fifteenth century timber-framed building, originally having a central hall open to the roof, and two crosswings. A floor was inserted in the hall in the late-sixteenth century, and there were other later alterations. It was occupied in 1910 (about the date of this photograph), by Herbert Cole, and was demolished about 1940, although a barn was still standing in 1951.

HIGH STREET GRAYS

26. HIGH STREET, GRAYS. In this view of the northern half of Grays High Street we see the range of shops common to most small towns, but this postcard is particularly valuable for its record of the Empire Theatre with its impressive entrance, and decorative panels proclaiming 'Comedy, Tragedy, Opera'. It opened in December 1910, so could not have been very old when this picture was taken. During its first five years the 800 seat theatre was used mainly as a cinema, but from the end of 1915 variety performances were presented, and several stars of the Music Hall appeared there, including, in February 1916, the celebrated Marie Lloyd.

59319. HORNDON ON THE HILL

27. HORNDON-ON-THE-HILL. An unusual view of the village of Horndon which could not be reproduced today. The mill has gone, although the remains of its brick base can be found in the centre of a small housing development, while the yard buildings and pond have completely disappeared. It is clear from the dilapidated condition of the mill that it had ceased to operate by the time this picture was taken, probably about 1910. The church with its characteristic spire has of course survived. Dedicated to Saints Peter and Paul, it dates mainly from the thirteenth century and is full of interest for the visitor.

28. TILBURY DOCK. This 1920's photograph of Tilbury Dock reminds us of the extent to which goods were loaded and unloaded by hand before the development of modern container systems. Along the railway-track on the right-hand side of the dock can be seen the bases of huge cranes which were part of the original dock installations and were illustrated in a brochure produced for the opening of the dock in 1886. The Liverpool registered ship 'Malakand', moored on this side of the dock, was named after a province of Pakistan. It was built in 1919 for the Brocklebank Company which had a long association with Tilbury.

BELHUR PARK. AVELEY.

29. BELHUS PARK. This view of the house and park at Belhus (with an interesting misprint) was probably taken during the 1930's. Essentially a Tudor building with mediaeval origins and eighteenth century alterations, Belhus was the home of the Barrett and Barrett-Lennard families from the fourteenth century until the estate was sold to The Thames Land Company in 1922. Occupation by the army between 1939 and 1945 resulted in damage which was one of several factors leading to the demolition of the house in 1956. The grounds, which were landscaped by 'Capability' Brown in the eighteenth century, survive as a public park and golf course.

30. FORMAL GROUP AT BELHUS. Taken around 1900, this photograph shows Sir Thomas Barrett-Lennard surrounded by his immediate family and a party of guests, including the tenants of farms on the extensive Belhus Estate. They are standing outside the main entrance on the west side of the house, beneath the family coat of arms. The wire-protected windows of the entrance hall were filled with stained and painted glass recording in heraldic form the marriages and other family connections of the Barrett-Lennards. This ancient glass was sold to a collector in 1922, and was eventually used to decorate a Tudor-style house in America.

31. RAILWAY CROSSING AT PURFLEET. Mrs. Gifford, the wife of the level crossing-keeper at Purfleet, stands outside a part of her house which has clearly been converted into a small tea-room and shop. Purfleet has already been mentioned as a popular excursion destination, and this establishment was obviously well placed to catch the visitors as they arrived on the train. We can see on its walls a collection of 'lucky' horse-shoes shed by cart horses as they passed over the crossing, and in the far distance it is clear that modern industry is already well established.

PART OF THE CROWD WAITING FOR THE VOLUNTEERS TO PASS 1·9·14

32. WAITING FOR THE VOLUNTEERS, GRAYS. This is one of a series of photographs by Menlove of Grays, which record the departure of local volunteers to Lord Kitchener's army in 1914. As can be seen here, a large crowd turned out to cheer them on their way, filling the High Street from the Queen's Hotel to the Railway station. Casualties in the Great War were heavy, and many of the young men about to march into the picture did not return. With unconscious irony this photograph also shows the site of their memorial, which was erected where the horse trough and urinal stand, in front of the police station.

33. ONE TREE HILL, CORRINGHAM. The view towards the Thames from the slope of One Tree Hill is still a pleasant one, but is no longer so completely rural as it appears here in the 1920's. The river and the Kent hills merge into a skyline uncluttered by oil refineries and other modern installations. The horse-drawn hay trolley recalls a style of farming which was already giving way to a more mechanised approach. The names of the boys in this amateur snapshot are not recorded, but they are clearly enjoying a break from a task which, for all its picturesqueness, must have been very hard work.

34. THE WORLD'S END, TILBURY. This well-known local landmark was built in the eighteenth century just behind the sea wall, close to both Tilbury Fort and the ferry to Gravesend; a position which guaranteed its popularity with travellers, soldiers, and later with dockers. It was formerly called 'The Lamb', and although the date of the change is not recorded, the more picturesque 'World's End' was certainly in use by about 1850. In this picture of about 1919, the publican, Augustus William Easey, and his staff have come outside to join a group of soldiers. Part of a stable range can be seen on the extreme right.

35. HOMESTEADS STORES, STANFORD-LE-HOPE. A postcard that is interesting mainly for being ordinary, showing no picturesque scene or special occasion, but the corner store of F. Smee, built to serve the needs of the Homesteads development around the turn of the century. The card was posted in January 1910, and the photograph was probably taken not more than a year or two earlier. The store has the usual advertisements for well-known products of the time such as Lyons' tea and White's ginger beer, while to the right of the picture is a makeshift wooden sign for the newly constructed First Avenue.

36. CORONATION CELEBRATIONS AT PURFLEET, 1911. Every village found its own way of celebrating such events of national importance. The scéne here is 'The Dipping', one of the older chalk excavations at Purfleet which came to be used as a kind of village green and recreation ground. The Union Flag has just been unfurled to the sound of loyal cheers from the assembled company, which includes the boys of the training ship 'Cornwall'. In the background a strange two-tone block of chalk and gravel shows the original ground level in this, the first part of Thurrock to suffer from large scale chalk-digging.

37. POST OFFICE AT WEST TILBURY. The West Tilbury post office was already 100 years old when this photograph was taken about 1905. The tall yellow-brick shop was originally known as Quinton's, and did not take over the postal trade from the nearby 'King's Head' public house until the 1870's. At the time of this picture, the sub-postmaster was W.H. Hart who later migrated to Canada where he died, aged 82, in 1920. In Rectory Road several boys are standing in front of their village school which had been built in 1876 and enlarged in 1894. The schoolmistress in 1905 was Miss Jane Boyle.

38. LITTLE THURROCK SCHOOL. What a pleasant change to find that the photographer has taken his camera inside the classroom rather than lining up the children in the playground. There is much here that is typical of a village school in the 1920's: the building itself, already old, with its tiled walls and parquet floor, the wooden double desks with folding seats, and the rigid separation of boys and girls within the room. The children's clothes are also interesting, ranging from the scruffy to the smart, and including the girls' high boots so popular at the time.

39. JOYES' SALE, GRAYS. A.E. Joyes' department store at 4 and 6 New Road, was for many years the only one of its type in the town. Their January sale was a major event for local shoppers in the years before the Great War, and Joyes' were particularly adventurous in their pre-sale advertising, producing colourful posters which offered discounts and prizes to customers. Their January 1905 poster offers bargains in 'Ladies and Gentlemen's hosiery, flannels and flannellettes, dress materials and baby clothes'; it also promises a treadle sewing machine worth £7.7.0. to the lady spending the largest amount during the period of the sale.

40. DRAPERY DEPARTMENT AT JOYES'. Joyes' stocked a wide range of goods, including furniture, but were probably best known for their drapery department, shown here in the 1920's. This is a carefully arranged picture, but nevertheless records a more leisurely style of shopping, with chairs provided for the customers, and helpful assistants in attendance. There are also some interesting price tickets to be seen, including a down quilt on the right at 35/6. Joyes' continued trading on this site until the mid-1970's, and in 1984 the building was still in use as a furniture shop and indoor market.

41. THE CYCLISTS' REST, STANFORD-LE-HOPE. Cycling became a popular pastime during the Edwardian period with the result that cafés and guest houses were established in many country villages to cater for the needs of cyclists. This picture shows C.M. Medcalf's 'The Cyclists' Rest' at Stanford-le-Hope, where a large party of young men and women have gathered at Whitsun in 1909. A sign by the door offers Tea, Coffee and Cocoa, while another board makes it clear that those who travel by motor or horse power can also be accommodated. Notice the flagpole with two flags flying: a particularly effective piece of advertising.

High Street, Aveley.

Published by
W. Finbow
Aveley.

2.

42. HIGH STREET, AVELEY. An interesting view of Aveley High Street showing several buildings, but we are intended to notice particularly the two shops of W. Finbow who was the publisher of the card. Finbows had been trading in the village for some time when this picture was taken shortly after 1900. With a grocer's and general store on the left, and a draper's and chemist's three doors away on the right, they must have catered for many of the needs of the local population. W. Finbow published a series of views of Aveley which he no doubt sold from his shops along with everything else.

43. TORONTO ROAD, TILBURY. It does seem that in the great days of the picture postcard, no street scene was too boring to be photographed. We are grateful now for the record of these very ordinary scenes even though we may wonder why they were thought saleable at the time. Here the photographer has at least gathered an assortment of local children to add interest to a particularly drab terrace. This is one of several roads in Tilbury which date from the end of the last century and recall through their names, the town's maritime connections with far distant parts of the British Empire.

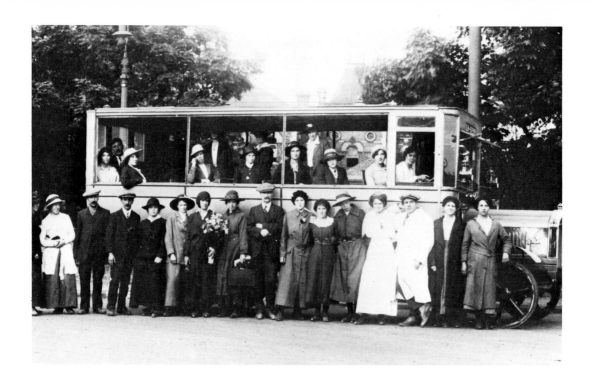

44. COACH EXCURSION AT GRAYS. A picture taken about 1920 by the entrance to Palmer's College at Grays. Most local readers will recognise in the distance the distinctive and once-familiar outline of the school buildings. The solid tyred motor-coach was one of the first of its type to be operated in the town. Details of this particular excursion are not recorded, but the coach is certainly a fine early example of a form of popular transport which was to be further developed in the 1930's. The white-coated driver seems to have abandoned his seat for a more prominent place in the picture.

Trinity Cottages
Mucking

45. TRINITY COTTAGES, MUCKING. Few people will remember this solid-looking pair of white painted cottages on the marshes. They were built, possibly in the 1850's, by the Corporation of Trinity House in that weather-resistant style made familiar by their many navigation stations. These were the homes of men who operated and maintained the Mucking Light which stood in the river on a 71 feet high tripod, and was connected to the shore by a long gantry. The light collapsed shortly after the severe floods of 1953 and was not replaced. This photograph of about 1910 shows the north side of the cottages.

THE BEACH. GRAYS

X.1017

46. GRAYS BEACH. Of a number of available photographs of Grays beach, this one best records the atmosphere of the place shortly after its opening as a pleasure beach in July 1906. The development was part of a bold attempt to create a seaside atmosphere on the Grays riverside, which involved the construction of gardens, a boating lake, and a swimming pool. The sandy beach was kept in place by a low wall, but nevertheless needed continual replenishment with bargeloads of fine sand from the East Coast. Open air band concerts and other entertainments helped to maintain the seaside illusion.

47. **FIRE AT ORSETT CHURCH.** The church, unfortunately, is almost completely obscured by trees, but there is plenty of human and mechanical interest in this picture of the volunteer fire brigade and their fire engine. Both Orsett and Tilbury brigades were in attendance at the fire in July 1926, which caused serious damage to the church. Much of the roof was destroyed together with many of the pews and other wooden fittings. Ancient stained glass was also lost. The photograph was taken by Mr. L.W. Turner, an officer on board the training ship 'Exmouth' at Grays, and an enthusiastic recorder of local events.

PURFLEET SCHOOL GARDEN

48. PURFLEET SCHOOL GARDENERS. It was difficult to decide whether to include this card or another showing the boys digging and pruning; probably this one best represents their achievement. From about 1910, under the guidance of a particularly enthusiastic teacher, the boys' gardening class of Purfleet school established a reputation, particularly for fruit growing, which was more than just local. As the board in front of the table records, they won either silver or bronze medals at the shows of The Royal Horticultural Society every year from 1911 to 1915. This is presumably the 1915 exhibit, re-displayed on its return to the school.

49. THE COMMERCIAL HOTEL, TILBURY. This building still stands in Dock Road, Tilbury, but has been converted to offices. Built towards the end of the last century, the Commercial Hotel was originally run by the Olley family, some of whom no doubt appear in this photograph. It is interesting to compare this building with the opulence of the Tilbury Hotel. Not everyone could afford to live in luxury, and there was clearly a need for a more basic establishment offering simple meals and accommodation. Notice how the card has been overprinted with a rubber stamp to identify the place.

50. THE BATA FACTORY AT EAST TILBURY. An unusual subject for a card, but a valuable record of the Bata Shoe Company's factory taken soon after it was established at East Tilbury in 1933. The company was founded by Thomas Bata of Zlin in Czechoslovakia, who died in 1932 shortly before this, his first British factory, was completed. His paternalistic style of management was, however, continued by his successors who developed a near self-sufficient community with its own farm, and with housing, shops, a restaurant, social centre, and cinema, provided on the site by the company. In 1934 Bata workers paid 10/- per week for one of the semi-detached houses shown in this picture.

51. THE ROAD TO THE HALL, SOUTH OCKENDON. This pleasant scene was probably photographed by C.M. Ansell who was active in the area around the turn of the century. It shows the drive, heavily marked by cartwheels, which runs from the village green to South Ockendon Hall, originally a mediaeval building surrounded by a moat, and unusual for the district in being constructed, at least in part, of stone. Formerly known as 'Bruyns', it was one of the manor houses of South Ockendon, but was already in ruins by the mid-eighteenth century, and only its gatehouse now remains. A new hall was built nearby in the nineteenth century, but it is unfortunately obscured by trees in this picture.

Dell Cottage, Grays.

52. DELL COTTAGE, GRAYS. This attractive thatched building featured in several postcard views. It stood in a picturesque hollow formed by chalk quarrying, and formerly used for lime burning, on the east side of Dell Road. As well as identifying the road and cottage, 'The Dell' provided a name for the nearby house built about 1871 for the celebrated naturalist Alfred Russell Wallace, who lived there until 1876. The house still stands on high ground to the east, but subsequent building has destroyed much of the wild garden that Wallace created in the pit, and the drive that ran through it.

53. BEACON HILL LIGHTHOUSE. This is believed to be a final record photograph of this prominent landmark taken just before its demolition about 1920. The small lighthouse at the summit of Beacon Hill has an interesting history, having been erected, together with an adjoining house, in 1829 by The Corporation of Trinity House, in order to conduct experiments with different types of lamps, oils and reflectors. It appears as a new building in an engraving of 1832 and continued in occasional use for experiments until about 1870. Many an excursionist must have climbed to this point for the spectacular view across the Thames.

THE MONASTERY, STANFORD LE HOPE. 2439.

54. THE MONASTERY, STANFORD-LE-HOPE. Many people, on hearing that there was once a monastery in Stanford, have imagined some ancient mediaeval foundation. The reality is very different. This farmhouse and farm buildings were the monastery, which was not established here until 1905. The order was the Society of Divine Compassion, a group of Franciscans dedicated to practical work for the benefit of the community. They were particularly involved in social work in East London, and purchased the old Stanford farm formerly called Potter's Farm, as a country retreat, retaining it until 1947. The barn was converted into a chapel, and can be seen in this picture surmounted by a cross.

55. THE POLICE STATION, GRAYS. Two police stations have been built in Grays since this one was demolished. This building on Orsett Road, looking down the High Street, was replaced by another on the same site, which now serves as the magistrates court, while a modern police station has recently been constructed a short distance away. This photograph, taken about 1900, shows a typical example of late Victorian civic architecture; solid but uninspired. The Essex County Council arms can be seen above the main door, and a collection of official notices covers the gateposts. Once again, a group of children has been included to enliven an otherwise dull picture.

MRS TINWORTH AGED 100 YEAR

56. MRS. TINWORTH AGED 100 YEARS. What a lot of trouble the photographer went to, bringing the old lady to her front door for the light, and arranging the curtains to suggest a room interior. Mrs. Tinworth, of Dry Street Langdon Hills, was evidently the district's oldest inhabitant when this picture was taken soon after 1900, but it seems that there were others not far behind. In 1912, Horndon-on-the-Hill was sufficiently well-known for the longevity of its population, for The Daily Mirror to produce a special feature on the subject, which included photographs and interviews with a number of ancient inhabitants.

57. SOLDIERS AT TILBURY FORT. This is the most familiar part of Thurrock's best-known historic building, with added interest provided by the small group of men who occupied and maintained the fort in the easy-going years of peace that preceded the Great War. The men belong to The Royal Garrison Artillery, although only one of them appears as smartly dressed as we might expect. The stone-built 'Water-Gate' was built in 1682, and to the left of it is another seventeenth century building, a military alehouse known as 'The Sutlers House'. The fort is now in the care of The Department of the Environment.

58. THATCHED COTTAGES, STANFORD-LE-HOPE. These cottages stood in the angle formed by Corringham Road, which we see in the foreground, and the tree-lined Billet Lane which is just behind the right-hand cottage. At the time this photograph was taken, soon after the turn of the century, they were clearly regarded as a bit of the old rural Stanford, making a sharp contrast to the relative newness of the Victorian and Edwardian terraces and villas which made up much of the expanding town. The photographer was Drayton Wright of Stanford, a shopkeeper and publisher of many local views.

The Broadway, Little Thurrock.

59. THE BROADWAY, LITTLE THURROCK. The Broadway, not in fact 'broad' at all, is the shopping street established to serve the inhabitants of the many terraces that were constructed in the late-nineteenth century when Grays expanded rapidly to the east, eventually joining up with the village of Little Thurrock. Present-day postcard collectors will be intrigued by the window of J. Cummins' shop on the left of this picture, and would no doubt welcome the chance to buy some of his cards at their original prices of ½d. or 1d. each. Like Mr. Saxton of Grays, John Brough Cummins was also a hairdresser, the combination of hairdresser, newsagent, and tobacconist being not uncommon at the time.

60. SEABROOKES BREWERY, GRAYS. In this 1890's photograph we see the buildings and some of the staff of the well-known Grays brewery. We have no firm date for its foundation, but it was certainly operating before 1800, the company, to be on the safe side, claiming 'Established 1799' in their advertising. At the time of this picture, Seabrookes controlled and supplied numerous public houses throughout Thurrock and beyond, but in 1929 the business was sold to a larger company, Charringtons. The brewery was demolished in 1969 with the exception of the building on the extreme left which can still be seen at the bottom of Bridge Road.

61. OIL WORKS AT PURFLEET. A rare postcard showing the completely unpicturesque works of the Anglo-American Oil Company at Purfleet. The Company were clearly well established on their marshy Thameside site by 1895 when a directory entry describes them as 'petroleum importers'. In these days of bulk shipment and storage it is interesting to recall the days when 'a barrel' of oil meant literally a barrel, and was not just a measure of quantity. The Anglo-American Company supplied many an Edwardian motorist with their 'Pratt's Perfection Spirit', and eventually became part of the Esso Petroleum Company who still operate on the same site.

62. MOORE PLACE, STANFORD-LE-HOPE. This is one of few records of life at Moore Place during the time when it was managed as an experimental 'colony', actually a limited company called 'Production for Use Industries'. In much the same way that Potter's Farm (No. 54) became a monastery, Moore Place became the home of a non-smoking, vegetarian community, who put into practice the co-operative principles advocated by Captain J.W. Petavel, a retired army officer who was described in a 1910 newspaper article as 'the presiding genius of the place'. He was the author of numerous articles in socialist journals, and believed he had the answers to many of the world's problems.

63. CO-OPERATIVE STORE, WEST THURROCK. The Grays Co-operative Society, based at 68 High Street, Grays, had branches throughout the Thurrock area, and there are photographs of many of them. This one, the No. 2 Branch, was in London Road, and displays an impressive stock of groceries, particularly of canned foods. Posters in the window advertise bacon, butter, and the new season's jams, alongside the official notices which are probably concerned with elections or the payment of dividend to members. It is interesting to see the globes of the large gas-lamps which, in contrast to modern shops, would illuminate the windows from the outside.

64. POSTAL STAFF, BELHUS PARK CAMP. Belhus park, which has featured in an earlier picture (No. 29), took on a different appearance during the Great War when it became an army camp, and neat rows of bell tents appeared beneath the parkland trees. Various regiments appear to have been stationed at the camp, including the 10th Border Regiment and the Kings Royal Rifle Corps in September 1915. The large volume of correspondence generated by the many young recruits and their families at home was dealt with by these postal staff. They stand here around the camp post box where they have obligingly recorded details of the occasion.

65. PRIZE BULL AT GRAYS. This fine beast is held not by the proud farmer, but by the butcher, Mr. Charles Osborn, of New Road Grays, who has just purchased it at a local fat stock sale. The younger man by the bull's head is Mr. C.E. Osborn. A card hung round the animal's neck reads 'Third prize best fat steer'. Though a strange sight in the middle of town, it was probably not quite so strange in 1911 when this photograph was taken. The building in the background displaying a political poster on its noticeboard is the Conservative Club which is still in Clarence Road.

66. THE WATT FAMILY AND FRIENDS AT HEATH PLACE, ORSETT. In the last quarter of the nineteenth century, a series of bad harvests combined with a dramatic fall in world grain prices, put an end to the prosperity enjoyed by local farmers in the 1850's and 1860's. A consequence of this was that Scottish dairy farmers were attracted to the area by the extremely low rents being asked, and the prospect of supplying milk to London. Mr. M.B. Watt, seated in the centre of this group, led the way when he moved from Ayrshire to Heath Place with his family in 1889, bringing his cattle on a specially chartered train.

Post Office Langdon Hills.

36.

67. POST OFFICE, LANGDON HILLS. Readers who know the area will have little difficulty in placing this view on the road which rises from Laindon to the Crown Hotel, just visible at the top left of the picture. Mrs. Elizabeth Frith's post office and shop provided basic necessities, while 'The Crown', already established by the mid-eighteenth century, was a popular base for shooting parties around 1900, and although the sporting aspect has diminished, the area retains many of its rural attractions. A more significant change has been the abandoning of many smallholdings – generally unsuccessful attempts at self-sufficiency in the 1880's and 1890's.

68. HARDMAN SIGN WRITER, GRAYS. For a sign writing firm, the sign over the shop assumes a greater significance than usual, and here we have a fine example of what is now almost a lost art. The board stating 'Only Ex-Servicemen Employed' recalls the plight of many such survivors of the Great War in its appeal for sympathetic consideration. The photograph was taken about 1920 by the well-known local portrait photographer, S. Edwin, whose studio was also in Clarence Road at No. 113. His impressed mark can be seen in the bottom right hand corner.

69. EMPIRE DAY AT HORNDON-ON-THE-HILL. Empire Day, a public celebration of the British Empire, was inaugurated in 1902, and was held on May 24th annually until 1958 when it became 'Commonwealth Day'. In the early years the event was celebrated with great enthusiasm, parades and pageants taking place in towns and villages throughout the country. Among the more ambitious home-made costumes displayed here, a number of Horndon boys have conveniently become Canadians and Australians, making use of their Boy Scout uniforms. Baden-Powell's Scout Movement had been created in 1908, only a short time before this picture was taken.

70. THE TILBURY HOTEL. The Tilbury Hotel is one of Thurrock's lost landmarks. It was part of the original docks development, and opened on April 17th, 1886. The architect was Mr. E.A. Gruning, and the builders were Perry and Co. of Bow. Standing at the entrance to the dock, it became a familiar sight to travellers, and was much used for overnight stays by passengers arriving or departing on the many cruise ships which operated from Tilbury. The hotel provided facilities of a very high standard, and unusually for the 1880's, was able to claim 'Electric Light Throughout'. It was destroyed by incendiary bombs in 1944.

71. TILBURY HOTEL STAFF, 1907. This photograph allows us to see the people responsible for the high standard of service already referred to. Here are the cooks, waiters, waitresses, chambermaids and other staff, including a porter with 'Tilbury Hotel' on his hat. They have been arranged in the pleasant little garden which ran alongside the hotel, separated from it by a tall hedge. The manager at this time was Leopold C. Bentley who does not appear to have included himself in this picture. A well-known local personality, he was manager of the hotel from 1899 to 1926, and from 1904 was also a member of the Orsett Rural District Council.

72. STIFFORD HILL. This view is reproduced not from a postcard but from a large exhibition print in which the photographer has made various 'artistic' additions in an attempt to dramatise the sky. It was probably made in the 1920's by a local enthusiast and shows the lower part of Stifford Hill where the road turns sharply to the left on its way to the bridge over the Mardyke. The road has been widened and given a hard surface, but the thatched cottage remains, and the area still provides a pleasant rural interlude between the villages of Stifford and South Ockendon.

73. T.S. EXMOUTH AT GRAYS. The training ship 'Exmouth' is well remembered in Grays, and this is not surprising for although it left about the time that war broke out in 1939, the two ships named 'Exmouth' were part of the life of the town for more than sixty years. The 700 or so boys undergoing naval training were a familiar sight around Grays, since they came ashore regularly for games, swimming, and other activities. The ship in this picture is the second 'Exmouth' which came to Grays in 1905, and the photograph was taken in the early 1920's by one of the ship's officers, Mr. L.W. Turner.

74. CORRINGHAM LIGHT RAILWAY. When the Kynoch company set up their explosives factory on a remote marshland site in 1896 (see No. 97), they were faced with the problem of transporting workers between their homes and the works. The solution was to build a 2¾ mile standard gauge railway with a passenger station at Corringham, and also a connection to the L.T.S.R. main line for the transport of goods. The line opened in 1901 and was soon using two engines named 'Cordite' and 'Kynite' after two of the company's products. In the early days six passenger trains a day made the twelve minute journey.

75. CROSS'S PIERROTS, GRAYS PARK. Grays Park represents a late Victorian attempt to create an amenity out of a problem. The area was formerly a brickfield, where years of clay digging had produced a wide hollow. The park was probably about twenty years old when this picture was taken around 1905, and as the photograph shows, offered attractions not found today. Cross's Pierrots, led by Albert P. Cross, were regular performers on the small open air stage. A surprisingly large crowd has gathered to watch them, presumably on a Sunday evening (the performance began at 8 p.m.), with many apparently unable to get into the temporary hurdle-built enclosure.

THE GREEN WEST TILBURY.   1865.

76. WEST TILBURY VILLAGE GREEN. The large triangular green at West Tilbury may have been planned as early as 1257, when Richard de Tilbury, lord of the manor, was granted the right to hold a market there. Across the green is Bluehouse Farm which dates from the mid-sixteenth century, with a brick-built bay added early in the nineteenth century. The King's Head on the left is an eighteenth century building and was visited by the agricultural and topographical writer Arthur Young in 1767 during his 'Six Week's Tour'. The motor vehicle is from Pellings of Grays, grocers, who operated a delivery service to the rural areas.

77. G.E. CARTER, MOTOR AND CYCLE MANUFACTURER, GRAYS. A shop-front photograph of more than usual interest, mainly on account of the two motor-cars displayed outside the shop, and if vintage car enthusiasts have difficulty in identifying them, this is probably because they were at least partly made by Mr. Carter himself. Private motoring however, at this time, was for the wealthy few, and the shop's main business seems to be with bicycles, then at the height of their popularity. A 1910 directory describes George Everitt Carter of 60 High Street, Grays, as 'cycle maker', but also mentions his motor garage in London Road, which, according to his billhead, was 'open day and night'.

78. DENEHOLE DESCENT AT HANGMAN'S WOOD. We reach back into the 1890's with a photograph recording a visit by members of The Essex Field Club to the deneholes at Hangman's Wood, Little Thurrock. The Essex Field Club is an interesting example of the Victorian Scientific Society, having a membership with wide interests in natural history and archaeology. It is hardly surprising that they should choose to visit the deneholes, those deep shafts descending through the gravel and into the chalk, at a time when there was so much learned discussion of their origins. They are now unromantically regarded as a means of extracting chalk for agricultural purposes.

79. TEACHING STAFF, STANFORD-LE-HOPE SCHOOL. There are plenty of photographs of schoolchildren, but pictures of their teachers are rare. When we do see them, they add considerably to our impression of school life in the early years of this century. Here we see the staff of ten gathered around the patriarchal figure of Mr. W.H. Parren, the headmaster. He came to the school in 1892 and worked there until his retirement in 1918 when the Grays and Thurrock Gazette recorded in a tribute: 'a prominent feature of his school is the excellent museum of objects... probably the finest school museum in the county.'

80. A. SMITH, MILLINER, WEST THURROCK. This looks very much like the sort of shop that traditionally sold everything, certainly everything from cake tins to a new hat. The window display seems unbelievably chaotic to anyone accustomed to the highlighting of selected objects as practised by present-day shopkeepers. Mrs. Smith does not appear in the directories, but Mr. A. Smith, Grocer, had been in business at West Thurrock for some time when this picture was taken about 1910. We have the bonus of two interesting posters – a well-known pictorial one for Zebra Grate Polish, used for blackening iron fire grates, and a local estate agent's advertisement for houses at £236 freehold.

81. TENT MISSION, FOBBING. A rare photograph of one of the evangelical missions which roamed South Essex around the turn of the century, bringing the promise of salvation to many a remote village. The preachers' names are not recorded, but they seem to have been successful in attracting a large number of children to their open-air meeting. The texts, 'Flee from the wrath to come' and 'Look unto me and be saved', which decorate 'The Gospel Car', give a flavour of the message they brought. Notice on the left the small harmonium which would have accompanied the hymn-singing.

82. REED ROW, GRAYS. Only the older inhabitants of Thurrock will remember Reed Row, this long row of brick and thatch cottages which once ran along the south side of Orsett Road. Their thatched roofs gave a rural feel to what was already becoming an urban landscape in the early years of the century. The photograph is probably by Alfred Russell, a painter, photographer and musician, who was well-known in the town. There is some of his characteristic pencil work in the sky. In the distance is the distinctive shape of the fire station, more widely remembered as it survived until the mid-1970's.

83. FIRE BRIGADE AT PURFLEET GARRISON. These splendidly-dressed firemen were based at the Purfleet Garrison in the early years of this century and are shown with their equipment in front of the Commandant's House. Fire had been a major hazard at Purfleet since the creation of five large magazines for the storage of gunpowder in the 1760's following increased anxiety about the safety of the Government's powder store at Greenwich. A small garrison was maintained to protect the gunpowder and other explosives as they were developed. This fine Georgian house was demolished along with four of the magazines in the early-1970's for a housing development.

84. MURRELL'S COTTAGES, ORSETT. The lack of definition in this photograph indicates that it is not a commercial postcard but an amateur snapshot. It is in fact from the album of the Powell family of Orsett, whose pictures of local scenes have proved to be a valuable record. This view shows a pair of cottages on the south side of what was until recently the A13, the main London to Southend Road. It was taken about 1905 when a motor vehicle would have been a rare sight. The cottages are named after a previous owner, and have survived relatively unchanged in their greatly altered surroundings.

85. GEORGE STREET, GRAYS. The terraces on the north side of George Street, which we see in this photograph of about 1905, had disappeared by the 1930's to make way for shops and, in particular, the State Cinema which opened in 1938. The houses, however, are absolutely typical of their time and similar rows can still be seen around the town. We are looking in this picture towards the High Street which can be seen on the extreme right, and in addition to the interest provided by the children and their prams, it is worth noticing the milk-cart with its polished churn catching the light.

86. STIFFORD CRICKET TEAM. Once again, not a commercial postcard, but an excellent photo-graph of the Stifford team in the 1920's, evoking much of the atmosphere that we associate with traditional village cricket. We see them on their own ground at Stifford, presumably having just won in the local league the large cup which is so prominently displayed. Village cricket, like the football referred to earlier, was taken very seriously, and nearly all the Thurrock villages had teams. Results and accounts of matches were published regularly in the local newspaper.

87. THE PUMP, HORNDON-ON-THE-HILL. There must have been many of these cast iron pumps made by a London foundry to celebrate Queen Victoria's Jubilee in 1887. No doubt they were sold to parish councils throughout the land who were looking for a suitable way to mark the occasion. Water supply was always a problem in this hilltop village, and a visit to this pump, probably on the site of an earlier one, would have involved a long uphill walk with full containers. Nowadays Horndon has piped water and the pump no longer exists, but its memory is preserved in the name Pump Street, the road which climbs the hill on the south side of the village.

88. POOR'S COTTAGES, CORRINGHAM. This photograph of Fobbing Road, Corringham, was reputedly taken in 1894 and records two cottages which the Charity Commissioners in the early-nineteenth century had described as 'Poor's houses'. They were connected with a plot of land, the rents of which produced income for a charity providing fuel and potatoes for the poor. Parts of the buildings, particularly the chimney stacks, may date from as early as the sixteenth century. Rents from the cottages were 1/6d. and 2/-d. per week in 1914 when they were sold at auction to John Ransom, blacksmith, for £300. They were demolished in 1931.

Chadwell Road, Grays.

89. CHADWELL ROAD, GRAYS. This is another of those views that could be reproduced by a modern photographer without essential differences. The rows of houses, though altered in various ways, are still recognisable. The most noticeable change is probably one of atmosphere, the traffic-free roads of the early years of the century giving a feeling of spaciousness and calm rarely found in the area today. The instruction to 'drive slowly' hardly seems necessary. Of particular interest is the horse-drawn van of Pigg's Orsett bakery making deliveries along the road. This vehicle probably re-appears in the picture of their full fleet (No. 134).

90. FOBBING WHARF. It is still possible to walk out on the raised footpath across the marshes at Fobbing and look back on the site of the wharf. The main difference in the scene is the absence of water, since the creek was blocked near its entrance after the disastrous floods of 1953. Even at the time of this picture barges only had access to the wharf for a short period at high tide, after which the water retreated rapidly to leave a glistening expanse of mud. The barge in this high-tide view, of about 1910, is the 'Eliza' of Rochester.

91. CORONATION PARADE AT STANFORD-LE-HOPE, 1911. As we saw in the Purfleet picture (No. 36), the Thurrock villages were as eager as any to celebrate the coronation of George V in 1911. At Stanford, the celebration took the form of a parade through the streets led by the local band, so that this photograph of the event is also a valuable record of some lost and much altered buildings in the High Steet. Especially interesting is the elegantly painted sign at the entrance to F.E. Belcher's 'Providence Nursery', a piece of the country in the centre of town that we would not expect to find today.

92. MOTT'S FORGE, LINFORD. Posted in 1908, and sold by Joyes' of Grays, this is the only Edwardian card we have found of Linford, a small hamlet on the border of East Tilbury and Mucking parishes that had been known as Muckingford until housing developers in the late-nineteenth century decided they did not like the name. Mott's forge was situated at the junction of Buckingham Hill Road and Muckingford Road, directly opposite the 'George and Dragon' public house. The house and forge buildings still stand as a reminder of the rural past in an area that has been much altered by house building in recent years.

93. BOX DEPT. JURGENS' MARGARINE FACTORY, PURFLEET. This picture of Box Department workers at Jurgens' takes us back to the early years of an important local industry. Antoon Jurgens, a Dutch butter merchant, had been one of the first to exploit the invention in 1869 of a new butter substitute which came to be called margarine. Difficulties with butter imports in the Great War led the British Government to encourage the Jurgens Company and its rival, Van den Berghs, to establish factories in Britain. Jurgens' Purfleet factory opened in 1918, and in 1927 became part of Van den Berghs and Jurgens following the amalgamation of the two companies.

94. HORSE RAKE AT BULPHAN. This is another picture from one of those family albums which have proved so useful in depicting farm life at the beginning of the century. This snapshot shows Mr. Mee at work in the fields at Bulphan around 1905. Here he is sitting on a horse rake, but he also posed with other pieces of farm equipment about the same time. Kelly's 1906 Directory lists Arthur Percy Mee as farmer of Wick House and Hatch farms, and Mrs. Mee (presumably his mother) of Wick Place as one of the principal landowners in the parish. By 1910 he had himself inherited that distinction.

95. FUNERAL AT STANFORD-LE-HOPE. It would be interesting to know whose funeral this is; it must have been a well-known and highly regarded person to bring out such a crowd. Among the mourners by the church gate are representatives of various organisations including two firemen in their highly polished helmets. We also find that at least one other photographer thought the event worth recording; he can be seen with his camera and tripod in front of the hedge where shops were to be erected not long afterwards. The large house on the left, long known as 'The Doctor's House', has recently become 'The Village Inn'.

PALMERS' COLLEGE, GRAYS.

96. PALMER'S COLLEGE, GRAYS. The greater part of this solid Victorian structure could be seen only a few years ago, but it is now completely demolished. This was, in effect, the third school to bear the name, the first being a small building alongside Grays parish church, the gift of William Palmer of Grays, who died in 1711 leaving money for the education of poor children. The original schoolroom was demolished in 1848, and a second school was built in Orsett Road near its junction with the High Street, to be followed in 1874 by this third at the top of Grays Hall Hill.

97. KYNOCH EXPLOSIVES FACTORY, CORRINGHAM. This factory has been mentioned already in connection with The Corringham Light Railway (No. 74). In 1896 the Kynoch company purchased 200 acres of marshland for the building of an explosives factory. Nitro explosives, cordite, and various types of gunpowder were made there. The company's isolated group of buildings came to be called Kynochtown, being officially named in 1899 on the occasion of the opening of a school. With the declaration of war in 1914, the factory assumed a new importance and was expanded to cope with the demand for munitions, with women making up the greater part of the workforce.

98. BATES', MINERAL WATER MANUFACTURERS OF GRAYS. Boys searching enthusiastically in old rubbish dumps frequently come across the bottles of this Grays company. John Bates' mineral water works was in operation by 1886 when it appears in a local directory. An advertisement of 1898 lists some of his products: Soda water, Lemonade, Ginger Beer, Gingerade, Ginger Ale, Champagne cider and Orange Champagne. There were also cordials: Peppermint, Shrub, Clover, Aniseed and Raspberry, together with Wright's biscuits and Clayton's 'New Era' Beer. By 1902 (about the date of this photograph), the business appears to have passed out of the Bates' family, and Edward P. Caswell is listed as the proprietor.

The Rectory, Bulpham

128301

99. THE RECTORY, BULPHAN. This view of Bulphan rectory (mis-spelt Bulpham on the card), shows what would seem today an absurdly large house for the rector of a small and sparsely populated parish. Built of brick in the mid-nineteenth century, its pointed gothic windows give it an appropriately ecclesiastical air. At the time of this photograph, about 1910, the rector of Bulphan was the Reverend Theodore Alphonse Teitelbaum, the living being in the gift of the Reverend Walter Gough Littlehales, M.A., of Muswell Hill, Highgate, and valued at £209 per annum, including the residence and fifteen acres of glebe land.

100. JAMES CARTER, COAL MERCHANT OF GRAYS. There are a number of photographs recording the pride taken in their work by local traders. James Carter, Coal Merchant of Grays, appears here with his horse specially prepared for the occasion, and two young men who are presumably his sons, with perhaps a third member of the family peering through the double gates. The picture reminds us what a familiar sight the coalman was before the days of smokeless zones when coal was virtually the only domestic fuel. An interesting incidental detail is the wall on the left constructed of concrete blocks. These are early examples of a now familiar building material, and were almost certainly made locally.

101. STEPNEY HOMES, STIFFORD. In 1902, the Stepney Board of Guardians, purchased land to the west of Clockhouse Lane on which to build a children's home. Orphaned or abandoned children came not only from East London, but from other parts of the country as well. It was not a self-contained establishment; children from the home went to the village school, and the boys formed an essential part of the church choir. These links with the village continued until 1935 when the home was closed and the buildings converted into an approved school for delinquent boys. Since 1969 it has been a 'community home' run by the London Borough of Newham.

102. STEAM THRESHING AT HEATH PLACE. Steam engines like the one shown in this picture have a wide appeal nowadays. The various types of engine were capable of hauling a plough across a field, or, as we see here, of powering another piece of equipment such as a threshing machine, by means of a large belt. This scene of activity was photographed at Heath Place, Orsett, which is farmed now as it was then by the Watt family. Steam threshing was usually contract work, so the engine and some of the men were probably supplied by Mr. A.C. Cole of West Tilbury, the main local contractor.

GRAYS TEMPERANCE SILVER PRIZE BAND. 1932.

103. GRAYS TEMPERANCE SILVER PRIZE BAND. The brass (or silver) band tradition which is generally regarded as a north country phenomenon, is quite strong in Thurrock, continuing to the present day with enthusiastic local support for marching youth bands. Earlier this century bands were often associated with religious organisations and social reform groups like the Temperance Movement, which campaigned vigorously against the evils of drink, inviting people to sign a pledge to abstain from alcohol. This photograph, taken in front of the bandstand in Grays park in 1932, is one of a series of annual photographs of the band taken during the 1920's and 1930's.

EAST TILBURY SCHOOL

104. EAST TILBURY SCHOOL. Postcard views of East Tilbury are rare, so it is particularly satisfying to be able to include this picture of the village school taken shortly after the beginning of the century. The building dates from 1855, and, as with many of these 'National' schools, its religious origins are reflected in its architecture, with a gothic end window, a short spire, and flint rubble walls suggestive of a country church. The substantial schoolmaster's house on the left was clearly added at a later date. The school closed in the early-1970's, and the buildings stood empty for several years awaiting a possible alternative use, but have now been demolished.

105. HUNT'S FARM, WEST THURROCK. In 1906 John Hunt was one of the principal landowners of West Thurrock, though not resident there. His farm stood on the north side of the London Road, near the Fox and Goose public house. This photograph of about 1905 suggests that an older timber-framed building had, around 1800, been given a fashionable stuccoed brick façade, a feature observed on other local houses. The usual range of farm buildings stood nearby, and though mostly constructed of timber they included a mediaeval stone and flint dovehouse which survived at least until 1914. All the buildings are now demolished.

106. WEST STREET, SOUTH OCKENDON. Other pictures in this collection have shown the pictur-esque, rural aspects of South Ockendon, but it is interesting to see that even before the Great War some parts of the village were taking on an urban character. This row of houses in West Street (the road to the west of the village green), seem almost new with their clean brickwork and undamaged fences. A particularly attractive detail is the pair of posters on the shop wall advertising 'J. Bates' High Class Mineral Waters'. The staff of this well-known Grays firm appeared in an earlier photograph (No. 98).

107. VICTORIA ROAD, STANFORD-LE-HOPE. Though not a particularly attractive composition there are interesting things in it, particularly the workshop and yard of Mr. Brand. We can see him standing at the gate in front of a sample of his work, a glazed house door. The name Brand is still well-known in the town, but as an undertaker rather than a builder. The end wall of the adjacent house carries an enamel sign advertising The Daily Telegraph, which claims 'Half a Million' circulation. Further along the road is an alehouse sign, not entirely legible, of one of the local breweries.

108. LONDON ROAD, WEST THURROCK. Other pictures in this selection have shown the impact of industrialisation on West Thurrock in the early years of the century. This one, by contrast, shows some rural survivals in a part that we now think of as totally urban, the London Road. The weather-boarded cottages on the left, and the haystack standing in a field on the right, are a valuable reminder of the way things used to be. By the shops in the distance, with their familiar Edwardian advertisements, old and new forms of transport stand side by side — a horse-and-cart and a motor-car.

109. THE ORSETT SHOW. Not a published postcard, but a snapshot from the family album of a local farmer which records a private driving competition in the early years of the century. The origins of the Orsett Show, still an important local event, reach back to 1841, and a ploughing match held by the Orsett Agricultural Association and Labourers' Friend Society. The show was held annually from 1841 to 1879, was revived with new enthusiasm in 1895, and, with a break during the Second World War, has continued to the present day. Beneath the trees on the left is the display tent of Suttons of Reading, still a familiar name to farmers and gardeners.

East Street, South Stifford.

110. EAST STREET, SOUTH STIFFORD. A typical example of 'the corner shop', the kind of general store that was often incorporated in late Victorian terraces such as these for the convenience of their residents. The proprietor, William Everson, appears in the local directory for 1910 as 'grocer', but evidently sold a wide variety of goods. As with many of the pictures in this book we are struck by the unmade road surfaces, and by the popularity of cycling in the Edwardian era. In spite of these generally depressing surroundings, one of the young ladies in the group manages to create an air of elegance with her large hat.

111. THE PECULIAR PEOPLE AT STANFORD. Some of the older Stanford residents may remember 'The Peculiar People', a religious sect whose strict beliefs and austere way of life marked them out as very different from the rest of the community. The movement had been started about 1840 by James Banyard of Rochford, who was originally a Wesleyan Methodist, and eventually spread throughout South East Essex. Its members soon came into conflict with law through their belief in divine healing. In a number of well-publicised cases 'Peculiars' refused medical attention for their children and were prosecuted for wilful neglect. The movement still exists under the title 'Union of Evangelical Churches'.

112. THE FREE LIBRARY, GRAYS. Although it was replaced in 1972 by a much larger building incorporating a museum and theatre as well as a library, the loss of 'The Old Library' and its Edwardian charm is lamented by many Grays residents. The library was built in 1902 with the aid of a £3,000 grant from Mr. Andrew Carnegie, to the design of the local architect and amateur artist, Christopher M. Shiner. This picture of about 1910, shows that the building had quickly acquired a picturesque covering of ivy, and also that Orsett Road in which it stood, was still predominantly residential, particularly on its north side.

113. THE BLUE ANCHOR, WEST TILBURY. For those who have wondered about the derivation of 'Blue Anchor Lane', this picture provides the answer. 'The Blue Anchor' was part of an 'L'-shaped range of buildings erected by Henry Crampton in the 1820's, which also contained eight farmworkers' cottages. About 1850 Seabrookes' brewery purchased the public house and grocer's shop, and it continued to be licensed for over a century. At the time of this photograph, about 1905, the licensee was Henry Hunt who can be seen centre left with his hands in his pockets. He had originally come to the village as stationmaster at Low Street in 1872.

1ST WATERPLANE TO LAND ON GRAYS BEACH

MENLOVE

114. THE FIRST WATERPLANE TO LAND ON GRAYS BEACH. Although the title of this card suggests that it might be the first of many, it is difficult to imagine why aviators should make a habit of landing at Grays, so this first waterplane may also have been the last. The aircraft is believed to be a Maurice Farman seaplane which came into service in the summer of 1913. It probably belonged to the Royal Naval Air Service whose nearest base was at Felixstowe. The landing clearly brought a lot of people down to the beach, including Mr. W.R. Menlove, a local insurance agent, photographer, and postcard publisher.

FOBBING

115. FOBBING. The situation of Fobbing, some distance from the main roads, has enabled it to retain much of the rural peace evoked by this photograph. The children nearest the camera are standing in front of Hill Cottages at the top of White Lion Hill. Beyond the cottages, the dormer windows belong to Prosbus Hall, a sixteenth century building re-faced with patterned brickwork in the eighteenth century. Above the trees is the distinctive tower of St. Michael's church with a turret at one corner. It was surmounted at this date by a small spire, visible from the river and an important navigation mark.

116. PARSONAGE FARM, WEST THURROCK. A note on the back of the photograph records the occasion – the sale of Mr. Vaughan's working horses at Michaelmas, 1916. Mr. Vaughan kept a large number of horses (there are eighteen in this photograph) at Parsonage Farm, West Thurrock, mainly for contract work carrying refuse for the Orsett Rural District Council. The farm was immediately to the east of West Thurrock vicarage which stood across the road from 'The Ship' public house. The railway embankment in the background is that of the branch line to Upminster, this section being just a short distance from its junction with the main line.

117. STRIKE DUTY AT GRAYS, 1912. This fierce-looking police sergeant standing on the jetty at Grays is one of considerable number of police officers from other areas who were brought into Grays and Tilbury to keep order during the dock strike of 1912. There was great anger among striking dockers at the employers' attempt to bring in 'blackleg' labour, and this led to a number of violent disturbances. A traveller by rail from Grays to Tilbury at this time recalled later that in one of the carriages every window had been broken, and that at Tilbury station 'We had to walk through a lane lined with policemen'.

Horndon-on-the-Hill

118. HORNDON-ON-THE-HILL. An unfamiliar view of Horndon, looking southwards away from the picturesque group of buildings in the centre of the village. This is Pump Street (referred to earlier in connection with the village pump) as it descends steeply to join the main London to Southend Road beyond the trees. The picture offers a pleasant recollection of the pleasures of motoring at a time when there were few other vehicles to consider; notice the dust cloud thrown up by this car on the unsurfaced road. The card was posted in October, 1916, although it may have been published a year or two earlier.

119. SLEEPERS FARM, CHADWELL ST. MARY. The village of Chadwell seems under-represented among Edwardian postcards, which makes this excellent view of Sleepers Farm all the more interesting. The farmhouse, which dates from the fifteenth century, can still be seen by the now busy cross-roads at the top of Chadwell Hill. The barn, however, has been demolished along with most of the other farm buildings, and the spectacular wisteria has been removed. The flags, suspended above the road, are evidently to mark a special occasion, perhaps Empire Day or the 1911 Coronation. The photograph is by 'S. Edwin' of Clarence Road, Grays, whose real name was Edwin Smith.

120. STANFORD ROAD, GRAYS. A puzzling photograph until we realise that Stanford Road is an old name for what later became Bradleigh Avenue, one of the town's pleasantest residential roads, which connects Lodge Lane with Grays Hall Hill. The section that appears in this picture is the steep rise at the road's southern end where the telephone exchange now stands. The horse-drawn delivery van is just passing some of the first of the imposing villa-type residences to be established here; beyond these houses there would have been an uninterrupted view across land that was still in agricultural use. The photograph was probably taken about 1910.

121. IVY WALLS FARM, STANFORD-LE-HOPE. 'Ivy Walls' stood in Billet Lane, Stanford-le-Hope, until the 1920's when it was demolished and replaced by a new house on the same site. It was an attractive sixteenth century building with a good covering of ivy to justify its name, but is best remembered as the home of the author Joseph Conrad, who rented it from March 1897, to October 1898, at £28 per annum, having previously spent six months in a house in Victoria Road, which he disliked intensely. At 'Ivy Walls' he finished his novel 'The Nigger of the Narcissus', and his son Borys was born there in January, 1898.

122. CHALK PIT WORKERS AT GRAYS. The Thurrock area has a long history of chalk extraction, ranging from the deneholes of the mediaeval period or earlier, to the large scale excavation of chalk for the cement industry from the late-nineteenth century onwards. The industry has now declined locally, but there remain many quarries like the one shown in this picture. Here we see not only the ordinary working clothes of the chalk-worker in the early years of this century, but also the engine used to transport chalk from the face, and the funnel-shaped gulleys formed by the old method of digging chalk by hand.

123. MAYPOLE AT HORNDON-ON-THE-HILL. There remains some doubt as to the exact location of this cheerful scene, but circumstantial evidence, particularly that of the postmark, points to Horndon-on-the-Hill. The picture was probably taken about 1910, a time when there was considerable interest in traditional dance and song resulting mainly from the publications of Cecil Sharp, founder of the English Folk Dance and Song Society. There are various references to maypole dancing in the area and by 1919 Chadwell St. Mary had its own Country Dance Club. Credit for these smartly-dressed dancers should probably go to an enthusiastic schoolteacher caught up in the folk revival.

124. GRAYS CO-OPERATIVE VAN IN BRIDGE ROAD. Here we have another photograph with the impressed stamp of S. Edwin of Grays, the subject being a horse-drawn delivery van of the Grays Co-operative Society. The van's number, which is painted on its side, indicates that there were at least 21 such vehicles in operation at this time, as might be expected from other evidence of the Society's success. The location is easily identified as the Bridge Road entrance to Grays park, a former brickfield which had been developed as a park in the late-nineteenth century. Some of the large houses overlooking it from the north can just be distinguished.

125. DIVER AT TILBURY DOCK. This picture is reproduced from a small carte-de-visite sized photograph which was probably taken in the 1890's, and shows Mr. Mitchell who was the East and West India Dock Company's diver at Tilbury for many years. By comparison with modern diving equipment, this outfit seems very heavy and cumbersome, but probably represents the best equipment available at the time. Beneath the helmet stands a manually operated air pump which would have to be carried to the dockside. A brass plate shows that it was manufactured by C.E. Heinke and Co., Sub Marine Engineers of 79 Great Portland Street, London.

Old Church, Langdon Hills. 10.

126. THE OLD CHURCH, LANGDON HILLS. Langdon Hills has two churches – St. Mary's at the top of the hill, and this smaller older one halfway down the slope towards Dunton. The 'Old Church' of All Saints was constructed mainly of brick in the early-sixteenth century. There were later additions and alterations, but after the building of the new church in 1877, the old one seems to have been neglected, and by the time of this photograph was starting to deteriorate. It was restored in 1931, but by the 1960's was once again in disrepair. It was sympathetically converted to a private residence in 1975.

127. HIGH STREET, GRAYS. Most of the buildings in this photograph have been demolished. The row on the left, which includes 'The Bull Inn' and the Grays Co-operative Society's butcher's shop, was removed in 1970 to make way for a housing development, leaving only the Rising Sun public house and the former Perring's furniture store on this south side of the parish church. (The trees indicate the position of the churchyard.) The King's Arms on the right survived a little longer, but has now been replaced by a block of flats. The row of buildings on the far side of the churchyard is still standing.

128. MUCKING SCHOOL. This tiny schoolhouse in a corner of the churchyard was built in 1855 in the gothic style with imported Kentish ragstone, so as to be in perfect harmony with the existing parish church. There were two classrooms and the average attendance around the turn of the century was 37, mostly the children of farmworkers. The schoolmistress at the time was Miss Louisa Blaney, working no doubt with the support of the vicar, the Reverend Charles Richard Nelson Burrows, whose vicarage can be seen behind the school. Mr. Burrows was well-known locally as an amateur naturalist, specialising in butterflies and moths.

129. THE BELL, HORNDON-ON-THE-HILL. The char-a-banc outing about to leave one of the local inns on a day excursion was frequently regarded as a suitable subject for a photograph, since photographers could count on selling a copy to most of the participants. 'The Bell Inn', which appears in the background, is a building of great interest and antiquity, recent alterations having revealed features which were obscured at the time of this picture (about 1920). Three men near the centre of the group are holding a tambourine, a mouth organ, and a melodeon, to accompany the singing which has long been a feature of coach trips.

130. T.H. HALL - THE BROADWAY, GRAYS. Though it is generally regarded as part of Grays, The Broadway, seen already in No. 59, is actually in the parish of Little Thurrock. This prominent corner site at its western end was occupied at this time by Thomas Henry Hall, who is described in the directories as a linen draper, although his wide-ranging stock also included such things as wallpaper and linoleum. A large painted sign on the wall reads 'Depot for J.J. Rayner's Liverpool Brand Dungarees, Serges, Engineers' and Stewards' Outfits', indicating as we might expect in this area, his principal concern with clothes for the working man.

60923. FOBBING.

131. THE WHITE LION, FOBBING. The White Lion is still a popular public house near the top of the steep hill on the south-west side of the village, but additions since the time of this photograph (about 1910) have obscured some interesting features. In particular the space beneath the jettied or overhanging upper story has been filled. The building was originally a hall house, probably of the fifteenth century, with a central hall open to the roof and two crosswings with projecting upper floors.

The brick-built annexe was a nineteenth century addition, and according to the sign, once had a billiards room.

132. CYCLING CLUB AT GRAYS. This photograph is believed to have been taken about 1908, and shows members of the Grays Cycling Club standing in Hogg Lane, Grays, at the point where it was crossed by the track of a chalk company railway. Informal cycling has been shown elsewhere, but this is evidently a highly organised club under the supervision of the gentleman in the bowler hat. Notice the cap badges worn by all members and the horn carried by the man on the extreme right to announce their arrival. The fifth and seventh men from the left have been identified as Dick and Arthur Thurgood.

Purfleet from Beacon Hill.

133. PURFLEET FROM BEACON HILL. The spectacular nature of this view was recognised as early as 1830, when the topographical artist, W. Bartlett, made a drawing, later engraved, from almost the same position, showing the extent to which chalk quarrying had, even then, transformed the landscape of 100 years earlier when massive chalk cliffs fell steeply to the water's edge. The vegetation which rapidly becomes established in these abandoned quarries, was one of the attractions of Victorian and Edwardian Purfleet. The landowner, Mr. Whitbread, employed a gardener to maintain a romantic garden of wooded walks known as 'The Botany', and issue admission tickets to visitors.

134. PIGG'S BAKERY, ORSETT. J.W. Pigg and Sons have retained a shop at Orsett although their business empire no longer extends as far as when this picture was taken about 1920. These seven horse-drawn and two motor vans made deliveries throughout the Thurrock area and beyond, Pigg's being the first local bakery to deliver bread by motor vehicle. A 1928 advertisement announces 'Grocery, Provisions, Corn Stores and Steam Bakery' and in earlier years sausage and jam manufacture could have been added to the list. In 1933/34 Pigg's moved to a site at the junction of Lodge Lane and Southend Road, Grays, which is still known as Pigg's Corner.

135. CARNIVAL AT TILBURY DWELLINGS. Industrial cities like Liverpool pioneered the concept of tenement blocks or 'dwellings' in the mid-nineteenth century, and when the Tilbury docks were being constructed in the early-1880's, the Docks company adopted this same solution to the problem of housing large numbers of manual workers, constructing two four-story blocks. The normally grim exterior of the building is relieved here by the carnival decorations. On this occasion, about 1900, the carnival queen was Nellie Suggett, of Tilbury Post Office, and her maids of honour were Ethel Brown and Daisy Church. They are escorted by members of the Grays Volunteer Artillery.

ESSEX UNION HUNT VANGE "BELLS." I.

136. THE FIVE BELLS AT FOBBING. We have an interesting building and an interesting occasion in this picture of the meet of the Essex Union Hunt at 'The Five Bells'. This old inn is still a well-known landmark having become identified with the large roundabout created in front of it on the A13. When Mr. Sullivan photographed it about 1915 it was, like The Bell at Horndon, controlled by the Baddow Brewery. The local hunt, 'The Essex Union', derives its name from the amalgamation in 1875 of two separate divisions which had arisen in 1839 in a hunt originally set up by Lord Petre at Thorndon in 1822.